MANAGING YOUR PROMOTIONAL MARKETING PLAN

First Printing: 2019
ISBN 978-0-359-80536-5
The Education Station
1359 White Tail Ridge
Cedar Hill, Texas 75104
www.keisie.education

USING EMAIL AS A TOOL FOR MAKING MORE CONTACTS

A small group of people who are interested in some of the things you are promoting is much better than a larger group of people who are not committed to considering anything you are promoting

Introduction

In the world of high delivery options for people looking to make their mark in the business world, email is just one of the many ways to make a difference on the bottom line of sales and promotion. Because the endgame is really all about revenue, there are reasons why you should try to discover the different ways to generate effective correspondence that will drive business your way faster and more effectively. Remember, the better you utilize the tools you have available to you, the quicker you can see results.

The advantage of using a reliable tool like email, is because it is safe when you consider the average business person has at their personal disposal in the neighborhood of 500 or more contacts in their email address book. The good news, it does not have to be difficult to implement an easy to set up marketing program through the use of your current list of email contacts. The bad news, if your list of friends only sees you as someone who sends them endless amounts of spam mail asking them to buy something, then you are going to lose friends and potential revenues. So, the key is to work hard in your approach and make sure that you have the right distribution strategy in place. Without doing this, you will have to work continuously at getting people on your email list and keeping them there.

HAVING AN EFFECTIVE EMAIL PLAN IS GOOD LOGIC

Gone are the days when people had to rely on the old way of sending and receiving typed or written communication. Today, with the Internet, email is one of the simplest forms of communication in the world. Anyone who has grown up in the days before the information-age will understand why email is so valuable as a tool for communication. Like anything else, the first time you are introduced to new technology, like the first time you used email, there is a great sense of ease that you receive, and may recall feelings of euphoria to realize that email was one of the best inventions ever.

Something People Relate To

Email makes it possible for anyone, regardless of location in the world to communicate with anyone else. The old days of "pen-pals" is now technology driven so that there are no more geographical boundaries as was the case prior to the Internet. Designing an effective strategy for using email to promote and market any and everything from small items to large, from cheap to expensive, from common to unique is just a few clicks away from having your hands on the mechanisms that truly drive the global economy. This is why from a personal or direct marketing perspective, there may be few other ways to get the word out about what it is you want people to know about the products or services you are offering to them.

When you think about it, email strategies are print versions of the old television commercials that used to flood the airwaves. Email is in many ways more personal, more direct, and gives you as the promotion representative an opportunity to get your "brand" out in the world, with a small amount of effort. However, like anything today, email is only effective when it conveys the right message and promotes the right image you hope to convey. Simply put, there is still a bit of luck required if the message and image are going to reach the right person.

Time and Chance

Just like television, the right people need to be "tune in" at the right time, to get the right message from the commercial at the right time. One thing marketing analysts lament is the fact that it is really easy for someone to mark a message a spam, rather than taking time to read the message, no matter how good the product or service being offered is. In an age with so many gimmicks and bad marketing practices on the part of unscrupulous businesses, how do people know when they are being spammed or not?

This isn't only a concern for email strategies, but the same is true for most any other form of marketing communication, whether Person to Person P2P, Person to Business P2B, Business to Business B2B or Business to Consumer B2C. Because most people have to be in the right place at the right time there is always a chance that the message may not get delivered on time or even to the right recipients. There is some leeway when using email, but ultimately there are no guarantees that the best plan be successful without a little bit of luck.

Targeting Your Audience

By using a safe list of people, you commonly communicate with using email, you are targeting a group of people who already have a level of trust with you, and those who are truly interested in what you have to say. Make sure that you don't throw yourself under the bus by making the common mistake of putting your own self interests in front of the relationship that took you time to build with people. No product or service is worth losing your friends over. This is something that people going after the money seldom consider until it is too late. For me, if I am satisfied that I am using a product that is a "miracle cure," then I would have no problem offering it to people in my circle of friends that know me personally, and know that my testimony of the product is worth listening to or reading about.

This can help when you want to get a start on your own marketing strategies for a couple of reasons. First of all, when using email correspondence, you are not wasting large amounts of money on a marketing budget for people who may not have any use for the product or service you are offering to them. One of the largest problems in getting any promotion going is promotion or "marketing" costs of getting the word out about your product. When you are using your own list of people to provide your information to, you have a ready list of people who know you, and may have a stronger sense of trust for you personally, as well as showing some level of interest in the product or services you are going to promote to them.

Why People Will Read Your Email

The fact that friends are your primary recipients will typically keep your email in their inbox until they read it, rather than deleting a message that comes to them from some unknown source. There is usually no limit or location issue when working with your address book, since the message is going directly to them. However, as I mentioned, be careful not to drive away friends by making them "expendable" in your decision to market a particular product or service to them.

A final few comments before we get into the strategies for developing your plan to promote or market to people using email. While email does make sense to use as part of a business strategy, it should not be the only source of outreach you use when trying to set up a solid marketing campaign. Email is really only effective when it is used in combination with other resources such as Search Engine Optimization SEO, Social Media Optimization SMO, Pay Per Click PPC, and Ezine Marketing. There are a variety of free and for pay services that will help you get the right tools for the right job from the beginning.

Conclusion

The best email strategy will only work when people have a clear path to the end goal, whatever that goal may be. For this reason, you must ensure that whatever you promote, people have a trouble-free experience. This means that whoever the client is, close friend or not, you are providing them with an opportunity that best suits them. This includes sending them to a given website so they can examine the evidence for their self. For this you will have to have a well-designed website or blog where prospective customers can easily gather the information, they need to make a knowledgeable decision, and this is a must when it comes to making sure people say "yes" when they have the opportunity to get involved or not.

It would be nice if there was some magic formula for this, but more times than not, you will have to try your hand at designing several plans that incorporate different strategies for reaching your target market group. When you come upon something that works, keep it safe, and try to replicate the results on different groups of people. When you are able to combine a variety of tools in the presentation of marketing communication, your Internet marketing plan will most likely be successful and unstoppable. It is really up to each individual as to what the plan is, but this guide is designed to introduce several things you can use to get started.

Now, let's look at how you set up your first plan for reaching a large community of prospective customers using what is already at your disposal.

STEP ONE – THE BASICS OF YOUR PLAN

The first goal for any plan is to maintain a high level of quality – While email may be a cost-efficient way to reach people, there is no excuse for producing content that is less than superior for a target audience

Introduction

The first step in creating a viable promotion to reach your email contacts is to determine what it is you really want the potential audience to know. They already know you, so you will be relying on your personal relationships with people you have most likely been acquainted with for a lengthy period of time. This fact alone should scare you, because we never want to disappoint when it comes to dealing with our friends. Especially when the stakes are so high concerning the product or service you are introducing to them.

This chapter is the first step towards building a plan that you will be able to replicate over and over again to a small or large audience of recipients. It is really up to you regarding the size of your target audience, but whatever the size, make sure that you are providing the best and only the best opportunity for them. Int the age of the Internet, people have everything at their fingertips, so if you offer something to them, they will most likely have seen something the same or similar to what you are promoting. For this reason, you must be prepared to think outside the box when it comes to setting up a plan.

WHAT ARE THE LEGAL ISSUES CONCERNING EMAIL PROMOTIONS?

It would be nice if it were possible to send enormous amounts of email to endless numbers of recipients, but the truth is, you are not much different than the thousands of marketers around the world that all have something to sell or promote. Why should your friends treat you any different than they would one of the marketing sharks that send them endless numbers of spam messages regularly? This is a question you should consider long before you set out to type your first email correspondence. Think of it this way, "How would I feel and respond to someone who claimed to be my friend and then all of a sudden tried to start pressuring me to get involved in their scheme?"

First things first, for most people in the world, the laws are very strict for Internet marketing companies sending out "spam" to email recipients. What exactly is spam? The dictionary definition of spam is, *"a disruptive, especially commercial message posted on a computer network or sent as email."*

Today, there is a very strict hardline on the use of spam in many sectors of the world. In fact, in the United States, Canada, Australia and throughout Europe there are currently laws which prohibit the use of spam for marketing purposes whatsoever. This doesn't stop people from sending spam, simply because there are way too many email services to keep track of every message being sent out around the world. which limit the sending of spam.

An alarming fact is that as of February 2018 an average of 14 billion spam messages are sent to email recipients daily. Of that amount, it is estimated that for every 12.5 million messages received, spammer will get one reply. That might not sound like much, but the point is that the control of spam is far from a sound principle when it comes to regulating the Internet. According to some of the most recent estimates, about to 80 percent of all messages received by every person who has at least one email account, are unsolicited. This means the likelihood of your friends being bombarded regularly with spam is great.

So how do you set yourself apart from the millions of marketers who are simply playing the law of averages for reaching a target audience? This takes a good deal of practice and training to develop your own style for promoting your products and services in a way that is along the fine line between what is spam and what is actually acceptable promotion and marketing messages. With the current laws in place, large companies are at risk when it comes to sending unsolicited email to lists, they have purchased from third party organizations. Understanding the laws in your current location will help you know what to do and what not to do.

Now, in the next section let's look at three ways to prevent being guilty of the "spam scam."

THE OPTIONS FOR STAYING WITHIN THE LAW

Because the laws are becoming stricter with regard to unsolicited email spam, you should do your best to ensure when you are making an attempt to reach out to potential customers it is done through viable ways that are within the boundaries of the local laws governing the use of spam mail. The first list you are going to rely on is the current contacts you have in your email service. Many people have multiple accounts across several email platforms, so it is likely that they will have many more email contacts than the average person.

So, how do you reach out to someone in a meaningful way so as not to be intrusive or overbearing with the particular products and/or services you want to promote? Three things are most important when building your list of recipients, you are targeting. The next few sections will provide a brief discussion for how to reach people and how to do it in such a way that you don't steer outside the bounds of the law.

An Introductory Email with an opt in Opportunity

Remember, your friend's list in your contacts is the first group you are reaching out to. Think about why you want them to receive the email communication highlighting the product or service you want to let them know about. Typically, and opt in opportunity would happen from a website where the person targeted is given the choice to opt in as a selection to the type of service, they are interested in.

However, you are sending a blanket introduction to a product or service that will be used to gain the attention of your friends, giving them an opportunity to opt in to your email correspondence.

Since you are creating the opt in list as part of an email written by you, you have the opportunity to shine to your friends about the things you want them to know. Don't forget that this first contact is an "introduction," not a full-blown sale to people. You just want to share enough information so that they will agree to allow you to send occasional email messages to them. In other words, keep it simple. The process should not be lengthy, and it should include a simple check box or option giving their permission to receive your messages, talking about your products or services.

Once they do agree to receive your correspondence, their email address can be added to your email campaign. Remember, never just email anyone with a commercial message to buy something. This is the worst type of personal advertising and will drive your friends away quickly.

As a rule of thumb, creating an opt in list is relatively easy to do. First, you can easily manage it using your current email program. The important thing is to have a way to keep some form of record of the virtual agreements that people have agreed to. For this reason, there are some email programs that make it easier to generate effective opt in listings that will ultimately protect your overall activity in the long term.

The right type of opt in list can lead to a multitude of additional contacts if it is done correctly. It's not just about asking people to join up for receiving email correspondence, what you are doing is developing the first stage of relationship building with your friends that will eventually lead them to making a decision to join you in the promotion of the products and services you represent. When you are allowed to capture someone's email address through an opt in, you should be thankful they have maintained their trust in you, and are letting you know they will give you the privilege of telling them more about your products and services. This is the highest form of honor and compliment they could give you.

The next thing to provide to people when setting up the plan is to make sure the people on your list have an option for discontinuing correspondence from you should they decide it is not for them.

Include a way for People to Stop receiving Your Email Correspondence

This particular message is referred to as an "opt out of service" notice. In almost every country with spam laws, there are regulations requiring companies and marketers to clearly provide a portion of their message, giving recipients the opportunity to discontinue receiving your email. This is commonly located at the end of the correspondence; however, some cunning organizations try to hide this in different ways so that it is hard for people to locate and use.

The fact that it is required should ensure that each email recipient receives some way of removing themselves from the current list of people receiving the offer. This is why it is always important to protect your own interests from potential problems, by being sure your email marketing correspondence always offers a removal link.

Certain types of automated email marketing software make this process very easy to do. Most if not all the software programs whether commercial or freeware will allow the user to offer a personalized message that goes at the very bottom of an informational email alerting the reader to their ability to remove themselves from the correspondence list. The digital system then handles this fully, making it easy to manage your list and to add and delete members from the list as needed.

The Importance of Accurate Contact Information

This feature of protecting yourself and staying within the boundaries of the law is often overlooked by people who are less knowledgeable about what they do. As a point of fact, in the United States, the law requires that all commercial solicitations have some form of contact information on them. Why? This is designed to allow those who receive the emails to be able to contact a real person at a real organization to request removal from an email list.

This is easy to accomplish when you are reaching out to people you are planning on marketing to. All that needs to be provided is an email address of the sender's personal or business mailing address. If your particular location requires the use of this type of solicitation, then it is best to use it. It is always best to take the safe route before you find yourself out of business before you start.

Another way of ensuring you have covered all of the requirements; it is helpful to publish your personal or company contact information at the bottom of email sent to anyone. What this does is show people receiving your correspondence that you and your business is, in fact, authentic and this could help them decide to receive email from you, and perhaps even work with you in the future.

Conclusion

Knowing the laws and rules regarding email correspondence will provide you with a first defense against potential problems. Each of the sections above have been written specifically to inform and give caution to those who think they are above the laws regarding spam. No one is above the law and it is better to be safe than sorry before you find out that you have been operating illegally, and find yourself facing legal issues.

There is nothing to worry about just as long as you understand your rights as well as email recipient rights. Some people have strayed away from email marketing because they are fearful of the consequences should they be found guilty of impropriety. Some have done so at their own business peril and found themselves out of the particular industry before they even had a chance to make it work. The truth is that, once someone learns the rules, understands how to work within the parameters of the rules, and they get the process underfoot, they can easily manage email marketing methods without thinking about them.

There is nothing like having the feeling of satisfaction, knowing there is no pressure to conform, and knowing that the people with whom you correspond are confident in what you are sharing with them. This actually takes the pressure off, and allows potential customers feel better about working with you. They will want to engage with you because you have done everything in your power to do things the right way.

STEP TWO – THE DESIGN OF YOUR PLAN

There is no such thing as a perfect formula for the perfect email – whatever is genuine, authentic and truthful will work, regardless of the message

Introduction

If you are like the thousands of people who try their hand at marketing some product of service each year, you have probably asked yourself many questions, and most of them ending or beginning with "why." People are usually successful on both counts of doing something or doing nothing. Either position produces a desired result. To people who choose to do something, the opportunities are endless, and the rewards are yet to be realized. To those who choose to do nothing, the same old stays the same old. No goals, no hopes, no dreams for a better life, just what you want when you have no desire to do anything.

When it comes to the matter of opportunity, I would rather be the person looks at the glass "half-full" rather than the glass "half-empty." Face it, life is full of lost opportunities, and the things we really want can be easily achieved if we are willing to access our own personal motivation to succeed.

This section will cover just a few of the essential basics for designing your email promotion. Some of the things will appear to be obvious, while other things will be a little harder to grasp. As you read through this section, be sure to jot down any notes in the margins so you can come back to it again when you need to be reminded of something.

THREE THINGS MATTER, YOUR TARGET, YOUR GOALS, YOUR AUDIENCE

By now you have been introduced to a number of important concepts regarding the right approach to developing a workable promotion and marketing plan. It may seem like a lot to grasp in such a short space, but in the world of business, time is money, and in your case, preparing your email is paramount to finding the right people to join you in your quest for a happier and fulfilled life. We haven't mentioned anything about money up to this point, but now would be a good time to think about what it is you really want to achieve.

How to Hit a Moving Target

I have never been very good at archery. In fact, any game that requires a decent amount of perception and distance, plus having me thrown an object at a given target can lead to challenges for me. However, when it comes to working with people and understanding what makes them tick, I tend to be a much better judge of character. You are reading this book right now and I sense that you made it this far because you are interested in what I have to say about promoting and marketing yourself and your products to others.

To be honest, when we set up our first email strategy, it should be done with a clear target in mind. What is your end result? What is it you want to achieve in this first promotion? Do you want to reach one person, ten people a hundred people, or more? The target is never the same in life and when you consider doing an email promotion it should not be the same either. Whatever your target is should be what you build your plan around.

I cannot tell you what you should set as a target for your first email promotion, but what I can tell you is that whatever you decide to use as a target, include yourself as part of the equation. What does this mean? Like I just mentioned whatever we do will provide a lasting impression, not only of what we are promoting, but also of who we are, and what our own character brings to the table. Never undersell yourself in what you do.

I have seen people attempting to give a promotional presentation, and they literally come across as begging people to participate in their promotion, when all they had to do is present the facts and let the facts speak for their self. What I am trying to say is that when you put yourself in the position of the target you are attempting to hit, then you will understand some of the same feelings and emotions people will have when they receive your first correspondence. Remember, nothing happens without you being part of the equation.

Are Goals Really that Important?
Goals are an important part of any face to face, group or email promotion, and regardless of what is being done. Without goals to guide the mechanism, then it is like a ship without a rudder to guide it in the vast ocean. Goals drive everything you are doing in the promotion, from how to set up your first email to how to set up your one thousandth email. Goals will change as the direction you take changes, but they are an intricate part of the promotion and cannot

be overlooked.

How many goals should you have? That depends on the size of the target you want to hit. Some promotions need only one or two goals to accomplish. Other promotions may use multiple goals to achieve results. Remember, goals you use should have meaning and be achievable. There is nothing like looking at someone's first plan and find their goals are too narrow or too far reaching. For example, setting a goal of getting one hundred replies in the first week of a promotion, may sound good, but unless you are a big corporation with a large budget, then it is just something that is not likely to happen. On the other hand, hoping to achieve a goal of five to ten replies in a week might be more in line with the type of responses you can expect.

Are there any tried and true goals you can set for yourself when designing your promotion? Sure, you can set a goal of eventually earning some revenues if you are a motivated person who knows how to communicate effectively with others. Other than providing a little guidance on the type of goals people like to set, there are not really any tried and true goals or objectives for promotions. Anything will work if you try it, and nothing will work if you are the type of person that sees the glass half-empty.

The goals you set should be "realistic" first of all. Setting lofty goals is what every marketing rookie has in their mind when they begin a new venture. Being the best comes with a price, and to be honest, most of the successful people in their industry have made many more personal sacrifices than they would be willing to admit. Some have even lost fortunes simply because they realized that the cost to them personally just wasn't worth setting their goals too high. Remember, shoot for the Moon and you will in in the place where the stars are.

Having Your Audience Clearly in Your Sight

This is probably the hardest thing to do about setting up your promotional plan. People usually have a target they want to hit, they have a set of goals the hope to achieve, but unfortunately, they cannot gain a good understand of who their audience really is. Sometimes this is dictated by the type of product or service being offered, but sometimes the lines of demarcation are not that clear. For this reason, the audience in any promotion should never be under or over estimated.

Imagine you were selling Frisbees©. Think about who the audience you would market your product to? What would be the parameters for the particular audience you wanted to attract to buy your product? Would they be young, middle aged, or older? Would they be active in sports or someone who is a casual exercise type of person? Would they be able to afford the range of prices for the product you are marketing to them, if you have high end products you deliver to your regular clients?

These are some of the same questions that can be reshaped in any way you wish to address the particular audience you are attempting to reach in your promotion. They are important for a number of reasons. Without having a clear picture of who the audience is, it is impossible to gain insight into just how you are going to interact with the group of people you will be working with, regardless of size. For the email promotion you are trying to find the right group to use as an audience for the product or service you offer to them.

Focus on the wrong audience and your efforts will quickly meet with failure. Undersell yourself to the right audience, and even though they are the people you need to be reaching, they will not respond in kind due to your inability to win them over through your own efforts. Believe it or not everyone wants to buy something, what they don't know is what it is they really want to buy. When you have the right audience and the right message to present to them it is like a match made in heaven, and nothing can stand in the way of your success and their ultimate satisfaction that you put a product in front of them they are proud to be involved with.

Conclusion

Again, we cannot wave a magic wand over the email and expect it is going to magically convey the message we want people to receive. It will take hard work on your part to formulate the right plan with the right target to hit, the right number of goals to address and the right audience to reach out to. When things fall into place, and I am not saying they will always fit together neatly, I am just saying when they do fit, you will have found the formula for at least one promotion you can use. The amount of time you spend learning how things work depends on how knowledgeable of your product of service you are.

Things work well when someone is understanding and knowledgeable of what they are attempting to promote. In fact, the things I am sharing will work for any type of presentation, whether it be email promotion, one to one interview, group meetings or large presentations. Since the focus of this book is on email promotions, we will keep our attention confined to this area. Let me close this section by telling you I am confident that you can become successful in whatever area of excellence you wish to achieve.

All you need to do is have faith in yourself and your abilities to do two things; learn and being willing to change. Learning provides you with the background and knowledge to master any subject, the confidence to find things in your life that you can focus on as part of your quest for happiness, the satisfaction that you helped improve yourself in some way. Change is what we all have to be willing to do when we are faced with a challenge that requires to move away from what our comfort zone is in life. The best you can be is up to you, and there is no limit on where you can go if you really believe you can.

STEP THREE – THE IMPLEMENTATION OF YOUR PLAN

People will never know your brand if you don't tell them. You are not promoting email to potential customers; you are promoting brand. That's why the vast amount of email promotion never gets done, because people fail to promote their brand

Introduction

We have come to the part of the book that is the most exciting for me, and hopefully for you as well. You are at the doorway of opportunity right now and the decision is simple, do you stand in the door or walk through it? I hope you will take a short journey with me as we show you how to implement you email promotion by creating your first full-fledged correspondence.

Now, try not to put too much pressure on yourself. Not everyone will come up with the right thing to say or present the very first time, and that is what experience teaches us. We learn to remember the things that work and quickly forget the things that don't. As mundane as it sounds, I want to remind you again that everything you do or don't do is completely in your control. There will be no force feeding here, so take what you feel you need to get started and leave the rest for someone else if that is what you choose to do.

This section will be a bit longer for the sake of explanation, so bear with me if something that seems simple to you is being explained in more detail. I have to do this for those who may need the extra word or two to understand what we are doing. On the next few pages we will look at all of the tools you already have available to you.

IT WAS ALWAYS ABOUT THE METHODS

With any email promotion, there are numerous ways to get started. Some people may want to use several of the options, or even just one or two. The key is to make sure you personalize whatever methods you choose to match your particular promotional need. Ultimately, you have to ask yourself, "What will help my email recipients become potential customers?"

Consider the following opportunities you have to develop a solid email campaign. Chances are, it will take you a short amount of time to start implementing and benefiting from the tools included in the following sections for your own fully workable email promotion. The total number of messages included in a promotion should be in the range of five to ten, each sent on a regular basis to potential customers and clients.

Make Your Communication with People a Habit

There are a number of things you can do to ensure success for yourself, but none more important than regular communication. As someone new to the marketing arena, you should make it a point to start each day by doing to your email with ideas in mind for getting your daily messages out.

Because email has become so commonplace in today's world, it has even taken over the short phone calls people make to each other to check in. The same can be said about social media and SMS services like Messenger©, WhatsApp©, Viber©, and many others that focus on person to person communication. By sending out regular communication to your potential customers, it is one of the best ways to let them know what is happening within your group and also to let them know what is happening with the products and services you want to introduce to them.

With all of the available technology, people can now access their email on their iPhone or Smartphone using email apps. This makes it convenient for you to create short and to the point messages that will go a long way towards ensuring you are getting your brand out there for people to learn about.

The purpose of making daily contact with your email recipients is not meant to be a way to sell something to people regularly. Rather, your correspondence is part of the relationship building process. Remember, people like to work and buy things from people they know and trust. Regular communication with your list of email recipients is a way of staying connected. Even if you are just sending them a brief note, make sure your communication has links back to your business or product website to help with the promotion of services or products.

Why do people need to communicate like this? One reason for doing this is to simply keep the connection regarding the products or services in the minds of potential clients or customers. Regular communication allows the promotional team to let people know who the company is, and it helps to develop a long-lasting relationship with people on multiple levels. This is why when creating the plan or promotion make sure that it is something that has a regular component.

Whatever the plan is for regular, daily communication, one thing Is important to be aware of; never overdo the process by burdening people with unnecessary communications. As we discussed in the previous chapter, you do not want to be sending communications focused only commercial messages. These are sure to be considered spam. By any recipient. The best thing to do is create a series of regular, short correspondence that are light and simple. This puts people at ease and let's them know you are someone who can be trusted.

One key to providing effective and efficient communication is to make sure you always offer something of use, that has practical meaning for people when they receive your daily correspondence. Make it some form of material the person receiving the email can use for information. Another way is to alert the customer or client to what new or unique things you have to offer. If there is not a currently running special, just offer some advice or wisdom in the email.

This every day approach will seem tedious in the beginning, but as you become more comfortable with making it a habit, it will become more interesting, and you will begin to see people respond in kind to your communication. The best way to manage this type of personal communication is to use a simple email client that will allocate email addresses into the appropriate groups. Then, you can send out one email address to a group of contacts appropriately.

There is no need for a large marketing budget to provide effective messages to the members of your particular team. At first, there is no need to set up an email marketing program like an autoresponder. Whatever the email service you use, just make sure you are managing it in an organized fashion. People tend to find that when they are organized, they can use what they have at their disposal to send effective email communications.

Creating Opportunities to Gain More Connections
Developing the right promotional marketing plan will take some time. No one is going to come up with the ideal promotional plan the first time they set out to create their own strategy for connecting to a potential market. As you develop your own set of skills with regard to your genre of promotion, your experience using email as a method for reaching out to potential customers will increase.

Once you have mastered some of the basics about keeping up with the regular communication needs, you can begin to explore all of the options for using your messages as a lead generation tool. The idea is to start with a small group of contacts and allow this group to be your incubation team for developing additional leads. Everyone needs help at some time in their promotions, and what you want to do is take advantage of the people who are already reading what you have to say regularly.

Of course, as an independent promotional representative,

you are already at a disadvantage, compared to larger corporate organizations. Most often, large companies have whole departments that are in place specifically for the purpose of using email marketing. They usually begin by communicating visitors to their website after an initial visit. What they do not have going for them that you do is a personal touch. To larger companies, they may spend thousands of dollars on marketing every month just to recoup a small percentage of potential customers.

Since you are working on a limited budget and you are focused on personal marketing opportunities, the heavy cost for mass email programs is not the only way to go. Gathering email addresses can be an easy process, and it is accomplished in a variety of ways. First of all, the people you currently know have friends they email regularly, and you might just make a short appeal to your small group of contacts for any referral email they are willing to provide.

Remember, you don't want to come across as a spammer, so make sure you ask only for a few specific email addresses from people who are convinced that others could benefit from the products or services you are offering. This is something larger corporate businesses do with their loyal customers on occasion when they are trying to increase their email distribution. This is perhaps one of the best ways to find new customers and to generate sales.

Finally, when using this method to gather additional contacts and connections, keep a few specific things in mind. Make sure your attempts to collect email referrals is not perceived as spam. You already know enough about this concern that it should always be on the top of your priority list of things NOT to do. Also, make sure that before you send any referral communication that you have the permission of the people who provided the referrals. This is easily done in a disclaimer statement when you are requesting the help of others.

Using Regular Newsletters and Articles

One of the more popular ways to get information out to your email clientele is by using well written and prepared newsletters and personal articles. This will assist you in being able to provide the most up to date information concerning your products and services. How do you write articles that are informational? Most companies and organizations have lots of product merchandise information that can easily researched to create your own personalized version of the content.

This is an excellent method to incorporate into your promotional plan, because newsletters and articles only different from small messages in terms of length. Strategic use of newsletters and articles will usually provide your audience with more in depth information, and can be used to teach a topic concerning what you have to offer.

Why would someone want to use a regular newsletter? In terms of promotional marketing strategies, newsletters give a larger view of the particular organization you represent. This is good for a couple of reasons. First, it lets your client base know that you are part of something much bigger than you alone. Second, it can introduce a number of products or services all at the same time, rather than relying on several email contacts to do the same thing.

By writing a focused article on a particular product or service you have personally researched, you are letting your group know that you are more than a novice when it comes down to understanding the products and services being promoted. It also lets the group know what is happening with the product around the world. This is also a good way to alert the consumer of new findings or results about the efficacy and quality of the product, or simply to provide some other type of information.

Be sure that your email newsletters or articles are interesting to the reader. It should also relate in some ways to your products and services. For example, if you offer product information and research on your website, in which you hope the email contacts will sign up for a membership through you as the primary representative, then your email newsletter or article should relate in a meaningful way.

Also, you may want to use articles that provide helpful tips to choosing the right products for their personal or professional needs, and explain what the true benefits of the product is. Neither newsletters or articles have to be expensive, especially if it is possible to learn how to create them yourself using whatever word processing program you are familiar with.

There are a variety of PC programs available to help most anyone do this type of "add-on" promotional helps and guides. If you are someone lacking the knowhow or experience doing this type of work, then it is also recommended that you find someone you can outsource this work if you would like. Overall, by doing the work yourself, you may spend more time rather than money on the process.

One final point about generating newsletters and articles for your product and service use. Correspondence should always point the consumer back to the product or business website. For example, it should include a number of links (in moderation) to a host website or an affiliate link you wish the reader to use. The key to this method is to quickly get on top of the promotion by offering a useful and insightful newsletter or article that gets people to react.

Conclusion

In any type of product or service industry, customer service is rule number one. You have to make people feel comfortable about what they are getting involved in. having a "sales first" attitude will drive people away from the outset, so your goal is to use the methods that have been mentioned in this chapter to build trust. Little can be much when it is done the right way, it is not always the fancy or gimmicky things that will produce a connection. In fact, the use of gimmicks is a sure way to way to cause more people to hit the removal link on the bottom of the newsletter or article.

HOW TO MAXIMIZE RESULTS USING YOUR PROMOTIONAL MARKETING PLAN

Success is not about trying to create sales. Rather success is found in the creation of value for the end user of the product or service they are being introduced to

Introduction

Ultimately, the success or failure of any promotional marketing plan rests on your shoulders. Many people are defeated even before they begin developing the particular plan, they are interested in creating. Why? There are several reasons why people fail, but the key to any unsuccessful result is probably because lack of proper preparation. It could be said that many people plan to fail because they fail to plan.

What makes something like an email PMP successful is having the right tools and the best information available at all times. As we mentioned earlier, people know when something doesn't "ring true," i.e. something doesn't feel right about what they are being introduced to. So, to combat this the organizational representative needs to be mindful of the things I will share in this final chapter. Success is a real possibility, but it will take care attention to detail when planning and organizing your promotion. Here are some things you will need to get the most from your messages.

THE FIVE ELEMENTS OF CREATIVE PROMOTIONS

I recently watched a motivational speaker talk about why people fail to realize their dreams. He said most people have the idea of laying on a beach somewhere, working less than four hours a day, and earning large amounts of "passive" income. He concluded his remarks by telling those in attendance, there is no such thing as passive income. He was right, and while I could go on about his lament against "easy money" schemes, I would just like to present five of the things I truly believe will help you put your plan into action and get results.

What I am attempting to do in this book is show you how you can focus on a short list of things that will help you create attractive, appealing promotional marketing plans that can and will produce results with almost any audience. It is staggering to think that the number one group targeted for email promotions today is the Millennials. It is estimated that more than $780 million dollars will be spent by this group who receives email marketing. This is why I selected five of the key elements to discuss in this chapter.

There is nothing particularly striking or earth shattering about the five elements, but what is interesting is that they work when someone uses them properly. I have tried over and over again to replicate the things that work and discard the things that don't. Why? Because there are too many people who follow the beaten path towards what brings the same results, regardless of the success ratio they are experiencing. For this reason, I want you to focus on only five things to help you create a marketing promotion that will bring you results.

Element One – Know Your Competition

You would be surprised at the number of people in different multilevel marketing programs that know absolutely nothing about the organizations out there that are their competitors. One of the first rules about competition is that you have to know how to even the playing field. When people are successful, they have discovered what other people like them are doing and "copied" their methods in order to see how they work.

Knowing the competition immediately gives you an advantage, because when people want to argue comparisons, you will quickly be able to counter their arguments with facts that will make the marketing playing field the same. Talking to someone about a product or service, and having little knowledge of what is out in the market is like walking into a dark room for the first time and knowing where the obstacles are. You cannot overcome lack of knowledge when it comes to knowing your own products as well as the products being offered by competitors.

Think about this, what makes your product unique when compared to other similar products offered by other companies and organizations? What benefits of your products are unique to what you have to offer? While many people use the "price is too high" argument, this is usually they are trying to find and easy way out of the discussion, so it is best to keep people on track, even in your email marketing promotion. This is done by simply presenting the facts.

Element Two – Be Topic Specific in Your Correspondence

Way too many people who are new to any promotional marketing program, want to cover the whole range of products and services with virtually everyone they meet or correspond with. This is a terrible mistake and one that will quickly put you out of business. When making your initial connections with people, whether it is in person or via email is to keep things light and simple.

Remember, there is way too much information for you to share in one opportunity, so give your audience a maximum of two or three options. Really, there is only need for one option, "if I could show you how you can become successful in promoting the products or services I represent, would you be interested?"

The options people have in front of them will determine their responses, and without being pushy in your email correspondence, keep your goal one that focuses on keeping your message on target and specifically worded. The benefit of this is that people do not have to split up their response between several options in front of them. They only have one way to react to message you are presenting to them, and you are most likely to get better results in this way.

Mixed messages confuse people. What this means is that when the subject or focus of your communication with people is too broad or covers too many areas, people tend to quickly lose focus for why you are reaching out to them in the first place. So, a good rule of thumb is to just keep it simple, and offer only one topic providing a single message from the organization.

Element Three – Lay Out Your Email Content Appropriately

What you have to promote in terms of products and services will be judged for value and need based on a few things. In some situations, it is simply a matter of time and chance. In others people base their final decisions based on what they see and read through an email correspondence. This is why one of your primary focus topics should center around email content and the way it is presented.

Knowing what is best for someone comes down to communicating it in the right way through your written words. Many promotional sales people spend too much time on emails that are so long and boring that they begging people to close them and forget about them. This is the kiss of death for a PMP, and you do not want this to happen to your own email correspondence.

Any marketing promotional should not be perceived as a sales rap sheet. You are trying to communicate a message that influences the decision-making process people reading your email are going through. They already have a "no" attitude before they even open your correspondence, so ensuring that they stay on your email throughout its entirety is something to focus on when you are laying out the content.

Remember this, the email message is not just about making the sell. It is about building relationships. So, as you begin to prepare your content, think about what you believe the reader wants and what they are feeling when they go through the email itself. sales letter. Your email is a tool to get people to the product or service landing page by sparking a particular interest in something you are offering to them.

It is okay to suggest a product or service in your content if you are SURE the audience you are sending email too might be receptive to an offer. It is also appropriate while making a point in your email to ask questions to your audience that would give them an opportunity to decide if they want to make a purchase. Only make an offer to the reader that is relevant. Don't avoid the offer, and don't go on and on in your content delivery without getting to the point. This will result in better success for the products and services you have.

Element Four – Customize Your Email to Encourage Traffic to the Right Website Location

It is likely that the PMP will have more than one specific product or service being offered. So, when setting up more than one email client for delivery of messages, make sure you have appropriate landing pages for all of the associated content links provided to the reader. This helps when you are promoting a variety of products and services.

When you have several email groups for which you are running a variety of products you have, you cannot have one single landing page and hope that it works out. The problem is this, once a reader navigates from the email to the landing page, they may have no idea if they are on the right website or location. It is important to tract all of your links and landing pages to ensure they work properly,

BEFORE you send the email to recipients. This will prevent any mistakes on your part and ensure that the reader is directed to the landing page alerting them to what they are looking for.

The landing page and content are sure to guarantee that the product or service you want the reader to see will be seen. This is why your email correspondence has to be designed in a way that will ensure your landing page and content are specific to the email you sent out. One of the best ways of doing this is to have several landing pages. Then make sure that each page correlates with the email by mentioning the product or service you are referencing. If the email promotion is introducing a new product, the landing page should relate to it as well. This allows the reader to feel like they are at the right place.

Element Five – Be Creative with Everything You Prepare

Few people understand when they are first getting started with their promotional marketing plan that creativity is probably more important than anything else. Creativity is the most important device for success in any business promotion. When there is a low percentage of creativity, the promotion will be negatively received. In fact, there is a high correlation between creativity and success. Creativity is what influences how marketers go about sustaining a competitive advantage over their competitors.

It is important to make what you present to your audience is interesting, engaging and unique. Your promotional plan will only be as strong as your email correspondence. The goal of any campaign is to drive consumers to your products and services, and to establish brand recognition for the things you are promoting.

Creativity fills the gaps between people's perceptions and what the facts are. In life, creativity makes life substantially more interesting and fulfilling. Your promotion should embrace the concepts of originality and uniqueness. People need to come away from reading your email promotion message with a sense of connection to their personal and professional needs. As the promotional representative you need to understand that creative people find ways around obstacles because they see them as opportunities rather than obstacles.

Other Tips for Successful Promotional Marketing Plans

While it would be nice to have an easy one-list-fits-all approach in doing your promotion, the fact is that somethings will work in some promotions, but not others. It will require a great deal of work on your part to ensure you have created the most appropriate and manageable promotional marketing plan.

In order for any email to get responses for you, to get inquiries for your products or services, or just to let people know who you are as well as what you have to offer, your correspondence must be written effectively. Marketing professional who do this for a living have spent years honing their skills, but with a little practice it doesn't require much time to become an effective marketer.

There are some simple steps that should be taken in order to create that near-award winning finished email product. By taking a look at the content in this section, you will become more familiar with what the "pros" are doing, and then you can begin to establish your own set of skills for the work ahead.

Of course, nothing happens without your message getting to the right people who are interested in what you have. They are just waiting for the right type of message to cross their email, and it will influence them to make a decision to look at your products or services. The only thing that is important in any email is the message it gives to potential clients or customers.

There must be something of value people are receiving when they decide to open your particular message. So, you must make sure the message to the recipient is intriguing, interesting to the point that they just have to click on the link you provided for them to learn more about what you are promoting.

There should be no short cuts in presenting the message you want to convey to your audience. The reason why is because there are no unimportant parts to your message. So, every part of the email message should be carefully considered in terms of how it relates to the end goal. Ultimately, the results will be seen in the types of response you get from the people who received the correspondence. Here are some things you want to focus on when preparing your email message.

A Clear and Descriptive Subject Line

Nothing stands out more in most case than the subject line of your message. This short introduction to your message actually sets the tone for what people are about to read. Nothing in the message really matters if you cannot get people to move beyond the subject line without marking your message for the trash, or even worse, spam.

Remember, before you can convey any message to your contact, you have to get them to open the email. The number of messages deleted on a regular basis ranges in the multi-millions daily, so you want to give yourself the best opportunity to be a successful email promoter. People find hitting the delete button quite easy these days and you are trying to prevent this from happening to you. What are some of the common mistakes people make? Here is a list of some of the more common things you should try to avoid:

- Use of ALL CAPS – Never do this, because nothing says "I am spam" more than someone who likes to use all caps in their subject line. Driving people away right out of the gate will not lead you to success in any way, shape or form.

- Fake use of "Re:" – This speaks volumes about the low-quality efforts of some people who are trying one of the oldest gimmicks in the marketing playbook. Without a doubt, most people will know right away that they did not email you in the first place regarding the message you are sending them. This too, is a very old and overly used spamming technique.

- Catchy Phrases or Quotes – Another tactic used by some to try and get people think they have something important to say, however, it takes little time for people to quickly realize it is just another spammer seeking to push their wares.

- Use of Low Quality and Subject Lines – Many people have been exposed to the long, promise laden email subject lines that are quickly recognized as spam mail. Avoid being the person who creates this type of communication and correspondence with the audience you are attempting to reach with your promotional email.

- Vague and Unclear Subject Line – For any person with a promotional marketing strategy, the key from the outset is to quickly get to the point. When the reader detects from your first words that you do not have anything really worth reading, they are going to assume it is spam and move it to their email trash bin.

Now that we have had an opportunity to look at those things to avoid, lets list just a few that will generate the type of response you are seeking through your promotion:

- The Offer – Your subject line may contain a quick glimpse of the offer you have for people without being overbearing or pushy. Remember, you are building your reputation with this email, so make sure the quality of your offer is suitable for the audience and something that provides the readers with options.

- The Quality – Subject lines that provide a short fact about a product or service is an appropriate way to open your message. Just make sure it is brief and always focus on getting to the point.

- The Value – When you offer something that is a good to the reader, the subject line will ring of value in its message. People are looking for something more than just opting into another of the many lists they are already signed up for. Make your short message one that immediately lets people know it is value worthy.

The items you just read through are not a comprehensive list of everything you should be aware of, but it gives you a solid foundation for beginning to work on creating your first promotional message to send out. Give yourself time to learn the ins and outs of what you are doing and be aware of the fact that nothing will be accomplished overnight. Most marketing promotionals can take weeks and months before they produce significant results, but they will produce. You just have to be persistent and committed to seeing things through. Now, let's move onto the next section.

Using a Valid Email Contact Address

Spam mail is easily detected by one phrase that has become synonymous with low-quality marketing companies. I am referring to the infamous "no-reply" email address. What exactly is a no-reply email and why should it be avoided at all costs?

No-reply is a single gateway marketing approach that

allows spammers to inundate people with email. It allows marketing companies to blast email recipients with emails, and the recipient can do nothing to prevent it. Simply stated, a "no-reply" email means "We want you to read about what we are offering, but there is really nothing we want to hear from you."

One rule when designing your email plan, make sure your audience is not limited in their ability to communicate with you. The connections and contacts you make are building not only your own reputation, but the reputation of the products and services you are representing. The best way to do this is by providing an appropriate "From" email address that is authentic.

Ensuring that your email is traceable and represents a real person or company name will immediately add legitimacy to your correspondence. In the world of Internet protocols, generic email addresses are an instant and immediate indicator of spam. People see them and find the easiest way to ditch them, i.e. marking them for spam so they are always filtered out from their inbox in the future.

The best way to remedy this is to have some visual representation of the company name in the email address that is clear to see. Most email programs allow for changes to the email sender line, to make it whatever the person initiating the email contact would like. Because so many companies use the inappropriate "noreturn@yourcompany.com" email address, which is impersonal and annoying to say the least. The best way is simply to have a return email that can be reached by the reader. This way there is no confusion as to what the email is about and how to contact an appropriate email box if the reader decides to act on something they read.

Personalizing Email for Recipients

The idea of automated email scripts is scary to most people. This is because it requires time in learning how to configure email and also how to arrange it in such a way that it is effective. However, in the world of email marketing today, promotional marketing messages need to be personal enough that they appear to be coming from someone the recipient already knows and trusts.

One way of the best ways to make sure this happens is by personalizing each message so that it contains a special touch, such as using the recipient's name. by now you have already figured out some of the things you need to do to make your email more effective, so it will take a few extra steps to align everything to give it that personal touch you are looking for.

Remember, from the time the reader lays their eyesight on your message. you have about two seconds to convince them to keep reading. This can easily be accomplished by doing a simple but unique thing. The best way to keep the reader's attention is to use their name in the greeting you give them. In the beginning, this will be tedious and somewhat difficult because you have no automation software to assist you. However, in time you will be able to find the right tools to assist with your larger list of contacts and connections.

When people first begin sending messages, they have to do

the personalization of each message individually. Once an upgrade is in place for using an email marketing promotion, the process gets very simple. Most PMP autoresponder programs provide the user with very simple HTML codes and scripts to use to include the client's or customer's name in each email without having to input the information on each email you sent. This way it is simpler to use the records already provided to do the work for you. Start each email with a greeting using the name of the recipient. For example, you might use something like the following; "Welcome, John, to this month's newsletter."

The greeting is only the beginning. You also need to take into consideration the ending of the email. The second-best way to personalize email is to include a closing with your name or the organization name and contact information. Consider the benefits of doing this. If someone receives an email, they are not too sure about or where it comes from, but at the end of the email it says, "Here's to a successful day!" By putting a name and phone number with this information, they will think higher of that email.

When personalization is added to a promotional marketing plan, it helps give readers an instant reassurance that the email is not spam. The reason for this is simple: by signing a name at the bottom, you as the representative of the products and service are showing that you are a real person. That matters in the world of computer-generated emails more than you may realize.

Personalization is an important part of your promotional marketing plan, so don't overlook its importance.

Using a Style that Appeals

There are a number of ways to attract attention to your product or service. How you influence buyer decisions can be done in a variety of ways, but perhaps one of the best ways it to user the right style format for your email. What I mean by this is deciding whether or not to use plain text or HTML text. How do you make this decision?

First of all, think about who your potential customers are. Are they likely to have a reader that allows for HTML style email? Today, most people do have this. Since most do, you should be using it. On the other hand, plain text emails are something some people are used to and most like this format. For many opt in lists, you can ask which type of email they would like. Your autoresponder or email program will handle sending the individual the proper type of email for them at that point.

There are benefits to using either of these options in promotional marketing campaigns. For example, when you use plain text, the email opens and is able to be read easily, giving your product or service more of a chance to be reviewed when compared to a long loading HTML message that will obviously take time away from the focus of the message.

There is no question that HTML messages give you more options in terms of design. You can craft a highly attractive email design that gets results. While this is more professional looking, remember, when using HTML messages, be sure that you do not overdo it in the area of graphics. You can be sure that no one will wait long to see what your message is about if they have to wait "forever" for it to load so they can see what the email has to offer. They will close it and move on without thinking twice about it.

Other Issues You Might Face

Misuse of Images- Many email creators are guilty of not using images properly. Since most email clients block images received from an autoresponder service or a newsletter or other email, it is important to realize this. A full half of the target audience is not likely to see images when they open your elaborately designed email. Most of these programs have a default setting that, unless changed, will block images from being displayed in emails.

In order to use images, be sure that the content also displays information in the email that relates to the reader. For example, if you only send an ad that says you are giving away your informational product in an image, and half of your anticipated audience does not see it, you are losing 50 percent of your potential for reaching customers.

Targeting the Wrong Market Audience – Have you ever wondered why people cannot get others to try their products or services when they seem to be doing everything right? Well, one reason for this may be that they have mistakenly taken the wrong approach for the audience they are targeting. In niche marketing it is important not only to know about what you have to promote, but it is also important to know who else in the market is selling similar or the same things. The only way to know what works in your niche is to know what is working for your competitors.

It's okay to check out the competitors to find out what they are doing. You may notice what they are doing right: such as using specific marketing messages each month that seem similar. You may also notice things that they are doing wrong: such as using an unappealing font or design that really turns people off. When reviewing the competitors' products or services, try to remain impartial. Ask yourself, "Would I buy from this organization? Does their correspondence and content format make me want to click on their 'buy now' link?" If so, or if not, ask yourself why.

Conclusion

In the world of promotional marketing, it is up to you to give all of your attention to the details that will allow you to create the best plan for your products and services. Usually, trial and error are the rule when it comes to creating just the right plan to use. However, give yourself a reasonable amount of time to develop your skills. Within a short few months you should have the specifics of setting up one or a dozen promotional marketing plans that will bring you results.

Wrapping Things Up

Congratulations for getting through this book on how to set up your own promotional marketing plan. There is a sense of thankfulness I get when I realize we have helped someone else learn just a little of what they will need to know to be successful in their own promotions.

Now, here are some tips to building an effective promotion that will help you to get your message to the right people.

- First, be sure that you are using an opt in list whenever possible. When you are able to get people to sign up for your correspondence, they are going to be the most likely to respond to them. Plus, these are the easiest email recipients to keep from claiming the email they are receiving is spam.

- Next, never use any type of bulk spam email address lists from third party vendors. You can buy these inexpensively but they are highly risky to use and may get your business hit hard by spam complaints. Most internet marketers also realize that these are non-targeted emails, too, which means the chances of benefiting from them is very low.

- Finally, consider using email sending services, like autoresponders, to manage a larger number of email recipients. One of the benefits of using these is that it is possible to take advantage of the list management services you contract with. They may also provide the ability to buy targeted lists.

When it comes to using promotional marketing methods, the final aspect to do well is to keep up on trends. There are always new ideas and methods being designed. Be sure to watch what others are doing and try to make this part of your own practice. Chances are good you will find a range of services popping up to help you. Keep within the rules and chances are your promotional marketing campaign will be highly successful.

www.ingramcontent.com/pod-product-compliance
Lightning Source LLC
Chambersburg PA
CBHW021040180526
45163CB00005B/2206